CORNWALL COLLEGE
LEARNING CENTRE

D1380684

JAN JANSEN

JAN JANSEN

TERRA

Contents

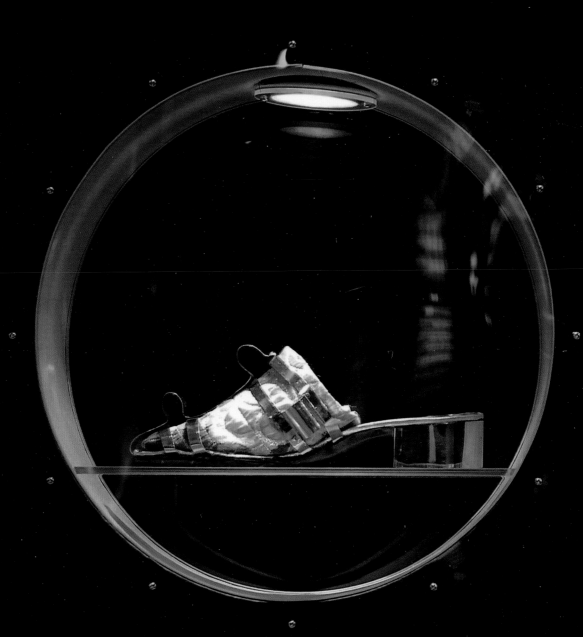

No.10
1967

Interchangeable 1
インターチェンジアブル 1

Foreword

What strikes you most about Jan Jansen and his designs are his incredible original-ity and his absolute determination to go his own way. His shoes are so convincing and full of life, and are always different. He follows his own dreams and does what he wants to do. He has no interest whatsoever in trends; no, he creates the trends! All his life he has followed this irresistible urge and inner need to make shoes. He simply couldn't imagine doing anything else; in fact it's what he has to do. Jan will continue to make shoes until he draws his last breath.

Jan Jansen is very famous in the Netherlands, but he has never built up an interna-tional business. This explains why he is less well known than he should be, given his creativity, talent and craftsmanship, and has never really received the recognition that he deserves. In interviews, he does admit that he should perhaps have approached the business end of things differently. That may be so, but ultimately it all comes down to his past and present creations; after all, his shoes are there. It is precisely his creativity that deserves our homage.

Time is my greatest enemy. I once read somewhere that time and matter don't exist in the hereafter. So you just think about something and it appears. Well if that's true I won't have to spend hours drawing and cutting out soles. Just think of the time that will save!

Jan Jansen

Jan Jansen in his own words

I don't often lose any sleep thinking about how I can stay 'fashionable'. I was once taking part in an exhibition in Copenhagen; people were saying that it was obvious that I was a Dutch designer, because 'The Dutch don't stick to the rules'! They had something there. If the Italian fashions are dictating square, round or pointed lasts then everyone follows slavishly. I take no notice. Some people in the shoe industry claim that I have been turning out the same old designs for forty years. Maybe I have, I'm still the same designer I was when I was 18, and I often do hark back to the

designs I created in the 1960's. Sometimes I go back to a thick wedge or a steel toe but always with a twist. It's very important to me that my shoes should remain timeless, so that you can't tell if they are from 1978 or 1992. My designs are sometimes humorous, sometimes naughty. Sometimes they irritate, but irritate in a good way! I include details that most shoe manufacturers couldn't be bothered with, such as putting a little heart under the sole that you could see only if you were walking

behind the wearer. I love that kind of thing, but fancy little trimmings are expensive and other shoe manufacturers turn up their noses at such frippery. Since I am my own boss, I can decide for myself what I want to use.

I often hear it said that I design 'fairy tale' shoes. People who are wearing my shoes can even pick each other out at a party. Can you imagine the conversations that have been started by perfect strangers coming up to each other saying: 'Hey, you're wearing Jan Jansen too!' My shoes also bear the hallmark of traditional craftsmanship. The fact that I learned how to make shoes by hand when I was in Rome has been of enormous benefit to me. Cutting and trimming, punching holes, endless experimenting, sanding the soles, covering, you wouldn't find a stylist who could do that. I am first and foremost a designer, then a specialist. When I have sanded the last, I always say: 'I've dressed you properly again.'

I don't read any of the marketing reports or fashion magazines. I don't study trends – I am always way ahead of them! My steel-toed shoes appeared well before the punk period. I was the first to design wedges. I actually predicted a lot of the trends. In the 1960's I made my wooden clog, the first Woody, which actually started out as a tourist item in a shop window in the Kalverstraat in Amsterdam, right next to the cheese and the windmills. Two or maybe even three pairs were sold. The Woody began to take off when Sophie van Kleef, the ex-photo model and clothing designer, wore them at one of her fashion shows. They were photographed and from then on the Woody was unstoppable. I was told: 'You really saw that coming, they will look great with the miniskirt.' But honestly, it was pure coincidence. People in the trade will say: 'Oh, don't bother asking Jan what is going to happen in six months' time, he has no idea yet, but he does know what's going to happen in two years' time.'

When I do have an idea for a design I see it as clear as crystal before my eyes. That's how it must be, that's how it must look and that's what I make. I can't tolerate anyone telling me that it could be different or simpler. Can you imagine anyone telling Dick Bruna that he should draw a bigger foot in one of his illustrations?
Ideas and inspirations come to me from the cosmos. I mean that, honestly. Suddenly there's a new shoe. Yesterday in the tram, for instance, as we were getting off I said to Tonny: 'I've got something, I know what I'm going to make on Monday.' When a design comes to me it looks almost like I'm having a blackout. I am literally 'out of this world' for a few seconds.

In 1962 my best friend Gustave Asselberg said to me: 'I think it must be wonderful to create something that no one else has ever thought of.' That one sentence changed my life; it's my unconscious motto, if you like. I love to surprise myself too, or if I were being honest, it's Tonny I like to surprise! She is my sounding board, my inspiration. It's Tonny who sees everything first. I create the structure and the outline, but it's Tonny who supplies the fine detail. She is the stylist and gives my work its finishing touch. With her carpenter's eye she can see straight away what would be better, but

Jan Jansen's first logo. All the subsequent logos were designed by Swip Stolk

PHOTO PAGE 13

Rob Aafjes

we don't talk about it then; if she doesn't like something then I can always go back, you see. Materials and colours, that's also Tonny's métier, she decides which shoes should be made in which material. We'll do these shoes in tiger print and those in some other, that's Tonny. She also tries on all the shoes that I make, and that's a crucial moment for me as I get to see what shoes look like on a real foot for the first time. Tonny brings my shoes to life, and she can wear anything from high heels to clown's shoes, from classic pumps to wedges. They all look good on her and it allows me to visualize the woman who will wear my shoes, having Tonny standing in front of me.

I always say that I must have been born in a shoebox. My father was a sales representative for Nimco, the children's shoe factory in Nijmegen. We were surrounded by hundreds of pairs of shoes in our house. During the school holidays I would wander around the factory and help out in the warehouse. Later I would make my first models there.

We had a good home life, money was never a problem. My father was already driving a car as early as 1947; it was an American model, the Nash. We certainly cut a dash in Nijmegen; almost no one else had a car then. My father let me drive a car on my fifteenth birthday. I used to tear down the Zevenheuvelenweg on Sunday mornings after church! Wonderful. 'Look, lad,' said my father, 'take a good look round, it's just as beautiful as Switzerland round here.'

My father didn't make any attempt to push me into the shoe industry. For a short while I wanted to be a trumpet player; I loved Louis Armstrong. I even played in a high school band for a while. Other youthful dreams included becoming a doctor or a clown like Toon Hermans. But that's all they were, daydreams that lasted but a moment. I knew deep down that I wanted to design shoes, it was the obvious choice. I remember telling my father about it in confidence; I didn't dare tell anyone else at home. I was so afraid that they would laugh at me; I was embarrassed to be honest. Silly really, but I think that it was because my sister was an artist. She went to the Academy in Arnhem. But my father thought it was wonderful. 'You have to do it,' he said. He never held any of us back, my seven brothers and sisters. Even so, this feeling of embarrassment was why I described myself as a window dresser for those first few years, and that's what I put on my business card: 'Jan Jansen, window dresser', a sort of diversionary tactic! I thought that putting 'Shoe designer' on my business card was just too presumptuous; it just sounded too 'arty'. When I finished my military service, I knew what I was going to do: they could laugh all they wanted, I was now going to call myself a shoe designer. That's when: 'Jan Jansen, shoe designer' appeared on my business card. It's funny, though, I have actually done some window dressing. Tonny and I once dressed the window of a shoe shop in Apeldoorn. This was the first time we worked together, we were already a couple. I was eighteen and had just got my driving license.

Tonny used to cycle past my house on her way to school, that's how it all started. I used to stand by the window waiting for her. Such a pretty girl who had already caught my eye. She used to wear these lovely blue suede pumps made in Belgium, and they were so much more elegant than the shoes we were used to in the Netherlands. We finally got around to making a date, and we soon found out that we were both shoe fanatics. We said then, and still do, that we are soul mates. My brown suede loafers, plus my yellow knitted socks made an instant impression on Tonny. We have known each other for forty-eight years and have been married for twenty-four.

When I came back from my apprenticeship in Rome, I set up my atelier in October 1963 in Amsterdam. The photographer Paul Huf phoned me one day, to ask if he could come and have a look. He was looking for people to photograph for his series 'Craftsmanship is Mastery', for Grolsch. Huf arrived and was so surprised that I couldn't count any 'big names' amongst my clientele. 'You ought to make shoes for Dick Holthaus' and Max Heijmans' shows,' he said. Huf got *De Telegraaf* newspaper involved and a few days later, there I was in a full page spread in the paper. The first sentence read: Amsterdam is richer by one craftsman. Suddenly there were all these other newspapers on the phone wanting to talk to me. Thanks to *De Telegraaf*, my name was established and I have the newspaper and Paul Huf to thank for what was in fact the beginning of my career.

The confusion of my name with that of the racing cyclist Jan Jansen has been with me for a long time. When he won the Tour de France, I hadn't yet become famous myself. Hundreds of people phoned me, asking: 'Are you the cyclist?' I should have designed a racing shoe for him, shouldn't I? Pity I didn't think of it at the time! I did design a shoe for the athlete Florence Griffith-Joyner, the Olympic champion, some years later.

Elvis Presley's 'Blue suede shoes' is world famous but I'll take my brown suede shoes every time. I have actually used blue suede, but brown is the colour for men. Men who wear brown suede shoes are always nice people. Look at Harry Mulisch.
An Italian would deliberately wear brown shoes with a blue suit. A Dutchman would never do that, he would wear black shoes. But Italian men only wear black shoes at funerals!
The best shoe-song has to be Nancy Sinatra's 'These boots are made for walking'. Music was really important to me and to Tonny in the 1960's. We used to go to

PHOTO Erwin Olaf

concerts, including one with The Shoes. Hey, ho what's in a name? I have made shoes for Robbie van Leeuwen from Shocking Blue, who sang 'Venus', and for Barry Hay from Golden Earring. When he saw my design, his reaction was: 'Now there is a shoemaker.' We did try smoking weed in those days, but nothing worth mentioning. Too little and in very small amounts – we didn't enjoy it much. But sitting in the Vondelpark with flowers in our hair, well, that was a different matter and we joined in wholeheartedly. I never went in for smoking; I'm more of a drinker. I was far too stolid and respectable, and I didn't want to risk my career and my family. You were offered LSD at parties of course, but we always said no. In those days I used to tell Tonny: 'When I'm sixty-five, I'll try an LSD trip – under supervision.' I'm sixty-five now and I still haven't done it!

Salvatore Ferragamo and Roger Vivier, two wonderful shoe designers, have influenced my work tremendously. Ferragamo's shoes were heavy and rather clunky, like mine. But I counterbalance that with my elegant designs. Vivier was incredibly elegant. In 1992, during an exhibition in the Stedelijk Modemuseum in Hasselt, I discovered that Ferragamo, who died in 1962 and of whom I had never heard at the time, had made a kind of floating wedge in 1947. That was quite a shock. I looked around a bit more. If I had found out that he had made bamboo shoes as well, then I would have packed my bags. I really would have been accused of copying his designs. Thank heavens there weren't any bamboo shoes in the collection!

I was also influenced by Dali. I loved his use of the surreal, and the craziness and sheer unexpectedness of his work. You can see the influence of his sofa with the lips in my erotic shoe collection, the Linea Erotica. The sculptor Henry Moore is another example – his stone is both hard and soft at the same time. Granite versus glowing, soft shapes. That's what my designs are like: too clunky and yet elegant.

In 1973 I took part in my first foreign exhibition, which was the Semaine du Cuir, where I showed my bamboo shoes. After that I was offered freelance commissions. I worked for the United States Shoe Corporation in Taiwan, for Caressa in Brazil, in China, Yugoslavia, Rumania, Spain, all over the world, in fact. These were all commercial commissions which I used to finance my shop. For the past few years I have been able to make a living just from my own collections. Thank heavens, because freelance work is now quite scarce. Everything is copied and designers are almost no longer necessary.

A few years ago, Tonny and I were in Tokyo when we came across a window display for Armani. There were my shoes, the Tutti Piedi! I was rooted to the spot. We went inside the store and looked closer and could see straight away that they had copied my design right down to the last detail. When we got back to the Netherlands, Alexander van Slobben advised us to do something about it. In Amsterdam, we started summary proceedings against Armani. We won, with the result that they were forced to withdraw the shoes from sale all over the world. I also wanted them to place a retraction in the press because they had used the shoes as part of their advertising campaign but unfortunately that was rejected. The Dutch news show RTL Boulevard asked Armani for their reaction after the hearing. They declared: 'An Armani shoe is always an Armani shoe.' Sour grapes, in other words. Quite by chance I know the Italian manufacturer of 'my' Armani shoes. He told me that the Armani stylist had bought a pair of my shoes on the Waterlooplein in Amsterdam. He made up a new sample and sold it to Armani as his original design. Unfortunately stylists do often pinch each other's designs.

An Italian friend of mine advised me not to start lengthy proceedings to claim for damages. 'There are two people in Italy who you should never try to sue,' he told me, 'the Pope and Giorgio Armani.' The irony is that I originally made those shoes in 1984 and no one wanted them. The Armani case was the first time that I had ever taken anyone to court. So many of my shoes have been copied – the High-Heeled Sneaker, the sloping zip shoe the Indian Boot, the Bruno, every one of them copied. In those days it was much more difficult to sue anyone for plagiarism and I just let it go. Nowadays it's much easier to take legal action.

Prada copied my bamboo shoes. Better that, I suppose, than some unknown Chinese designer, at least I got some free publicity out of it! But still, it rankles. I was at an exhibition when along came this large American who looked at my bamboo shoe and declared: 'Look, here's a copy of the Prada shoe already.' He simply assumed that I had made the copy, not the other way round.

My shoes are made in Italy and Portugal. Lasts, heels, models, everything is made there. I was in Porto this week to start on the first designs for the 2007-2008 Winter Collection. There, I have my own knife, pencils, pens, tape measure, file, pencil

sharpener and a plastic cutting mat. In Portugal I speak English; in Italy you have to speak Italian. I go to Portugal four times a year and four times a year to Italy. I also still teach in Milan.

I can't make a special last for each country, so I make an average last. I was once asked to make a special last for America. In those days, Americans had much smaller feet than the Europeans. They never walked anywhere, you see, they went everywhere by car. All that has changed in the last few decades. Their feet have broadened because now they all go jogging.

I can pick out your average Dutchman abroad just by looking at his shoes. You can spot a Dutch shoe anywhere, it's so easily recognizable. There's a reason why the Germans call us 'Bata men'. In other words, a cheap, unpolished shoe with worn heels, i.e. not looked after! We only have our shoes mended as a last resort. Italians on the other hand have their heels mended and polish their shoes on a regular basis; Dutchmen are much more slapdash. We are happy as long as the shoe is comfortable, while an Italian wants to look well groomed. I'm afraid that shoes come way down on the list of priorities for many Dutchmen. We're quite happy to spend money on clothes, but shoes? Oh dear me, no. Dutchmen, our 'Bata-men', eat hamburgers or meatballs every day, blissfully unaware of the existence of such delicacies as sweetbreads or a good pâté. Those blessed few who can actually see further than the ends of their noses are the people who buy my designs. We have one hundred and twelve clients in the Netherlands, and several abroad: in Japan, America, Israel, Switzerland, Italy and Germany. The Japanese really look up to Europeans. I have been appointed a professor at the Bunka Fukusogakin Academy in Tokyo, where I lecture for a few days each season. My students always ask me if they can take my hand, not to shake it, you understand, but they want to try to absorb some of my power. The Japanese really take their time when they are looking at my shoes, far more so than anyone else. They pick them up, turn them round and examine every inch inside and out, and with such concentration! What do they see, I wonder? Are they counting the stitches maybe? It's like they want to take a mental photograph of the design. An American will just pick up the shoes and ask: 'How much are they?' My style has really taken off in Japan, and I have absorbed something Oriental in my work. In 1975, my bamboo shoe was introduced in the Bijenkorf department store, but beforehand when I was showing them the collection, the buyer commented: 'Well, it's obvious that you've been to Japan.' But I hadn't – not then at any rate. Strange, eh?

I would love it if Princess Maxima had a pair of my shoes. I'm not too bothered about Queen Beatrix, but Maxima is such a modern woman. I wouldn't even have to design a special shoe for her, it's already in my collection: an elegant shoe with a very thin heel and a pointed toe, the kind that you often see worn by good-looking, well-dressed and fashionable women. We have actually had a princess as a client, Aimée

駐日オランダ大使夫人　ジュリ

鮮やかな青紫が目を引く「スティア・マイ・ブルー・ブラッド」

最新デザインの「ガーデン・オブ・エデン」。ジュリアンさんの心を打った作品でもある

お気に入りの作「フォン・レン2」の前で。ジュリアンさんの靴もヤンセンの作

ヤン・ヤンセン経歴

ヤン・ヤンセンは、19
41年、オランダ中部、ア
ムステルダムの南東約80
ロ、ドイツ国境に近いナイ
メーヘンの生まれ。父親は
靴製造会社の販売部長で、
少年時代から靴に強い関心
を持ち、父の会社で研修を
受けた後、靴の本場、イタ
リアでハンドメードの靴作
りを学んだ。63年にアムス
テルダムにスタジオを設
立、65年には、ブランドコ
レクションを発表し、
表、ファッション
雑誌、業界誌など
に取り上げられて注目され
た。68年には、ニューヨー
ク現代工芸美術館での展覧
一の名を不動のものとした
のは、73年にパリで発表し
た竹製のブリッジ構造の
モデル。95年には、国内、
ッション界でも高い評価を
受けた。
「ラッタン」で、以後、デ
69年の革を巧みに活用し
イオールやシャルル・ジョ
ルダンなど数多くの
の貢献に対し、名誉あるオ
ランダファッション賞を受
賞した。02年、ハーグ市立
美術館で40年の集大成の作
品展を開催、大きな反響を
呼んだ。芸術作品でありな
がら人間工学的品質を保っ
ている楽しい実用品の製作
を続けている。

出品、米仏などのファ
国際ファッションの世界へ
ランダファッション賞を受
ション流行の世相に乗り、
ーは、カジュアルファッ
ラ木製のサンダル「ウッデ
に展示されたアンクルブ
定して製造したアンクルブ
ーツは、最もコピーされた

芸術＋楽しい実用品

ランドからフリー
ランス契約を受ける。77年
の「ハイヒール・スニーカ
ー」は、時代のトレンドに
合って全米で100万足以
上も売れた。79年の数を限
り、独創的なデザイナ
世界各地で発売され、大成
功した。

ヤンとトニー夫人＝アムス
テルダムのショップの前で

この展示を見ていただき
いですね」
ジュリアンさんが特に推
薦する作品は、1974
年の厚底のスエード製ブ
ーツ「フォン・レン2」、79
年の鮮やかな紫のプ
ーツ「スティア・マイ・ブ
ラッド」、04年の
新デザインの「ガーデン・
オブ・エデン」など。
「ぐれたファッション性が
を打ちます」とジュリア
さんは、強調した。

中心地にあるヤンセンショ
ップで2足購入してきた。
お気に入りの靴を履いて
んにお伝えしたい。ぜひ
て下さい。それにはまず
お気に入りの靴を履いて
ヤンセンは、アムステル
ダム美術評議会から靴デザ
イナーとしては初
めて権威あるフ
アッション賞

「キス・ミー・オン・ギ
カウチ」、89年のかかと
浮き上がった状態の
ブ「スティア・マイ・ブ
の女性らしさが表現され
ー・ブラッド」、04年の
新デザインの「ガーデン・
オブ・エデン」など。

ヤーコプスさんが語る魅力

靴の魔術師
ヤンセンの世界展

ファッションの街、東京・渋谷で今、オランダのシューズデザインの巨匠、ヤン・ヤンセンの最新デザインなど代表作品130点を集めた「靴の魔術師　ヤン・ヤンセンの世界展」が開かれ、話題になっている。アメリカで100万足以上も売れる大ヒットとなった「ハイヒール・スニーカー」、竹を素材にした「バンブー・シューズ」、日本はじめ世界的な大流行の引き金にもなった「厚底靴」、靴の革命ともいわれ、業界では画期的な出来事でもあった「浮いたヒールのシューズ」、流線形のファスナー付きの紳士用アンクルブーツなど足元が輝くヤンセンコレクションのすべてが並ぶ。

オランダ大使夫人、フランソワーズ・ジュリアン・ヤーコプスさんは、ヤンセン芸術を愛するファンのひとり。日本初公開のユニークな作品が展示された会場でヤンセンの魅力について聞いた。
【鈴木義典、写真は荒牧万佐行】

足元で浸る幸せ

ジュリアンさんお薦めの作「キス・ミー・オン・ザ・カウチ」

シックでエレガントさが際立つフランス生まれのジュリアンさん。大使夫人とラジオの国際放送で活躍するジャーナリストの顔を持つ、スーパーレディー。夫の駐日大使、ヤーコプスさ

を受賞していることも、り、「ヤンセン文化」を本で広める手助けになれば、と考えたという。

「私の足にお尋ねくだい、と言いたいほどに幸つな気持ちに浸れるんですよ。この履き心地のよさな気持ちに浸れるんで日本のみなさんにも知ってほしいですね」

奇抜なデザインが目を引くが、足の健

んは日本に赴任し3年、夫妻そろってオランダ文化を日本に紹介しようと奔走している。

渋谷・パルコミュージアムを訪れたこの日のジュリアンさんは、黒のジャケットにヤンセン製作の同色のフラットシューズ、足首に結ばれた細い革ひもが光るオシャレな装い。渋谷の繁華街を歩いても足元に集中しているのが分かります。靴の話に熱する

にも気配りしたものがほんど。パーティー、イベント、会議などいろいろな所に出席するジュリアンさん。「今度は、どんな靴を履いてくるのかしら、と視線が足に集中しているのが分かります。靴の話に熱中することもあります」という。

大切にしているヤンセンブランドを7足は持って

靴の歴史上画期的デザインの浮いたヒール「ラブ」。

Candy Dulfer
and Jan Jansen
PHOTO Lok Jansen

Söhngen, princess Margriet's daughter-in-law. Especially for her wedding, I made shoes for Aimée and her mother. Several pairs actually, for the afternoon and for the evening. Her couturier had sent her to us, so that I could make the shoes using the same material as her dress. I received a lovely letter from her after the wedding, saying that she had been able to dance painlessly in my shoes for two entire evenings. That's because I had used thick foam rubber. This had caused me some headaches, I can tell you. Two days before the wedding, I received the shoes from the factory in Portugal, but they had forgotten the foam rubber! Total panic set in. I phoned the couturier straight away to ask if they still had some material left over. Then I had to fly back and forth to Portugal to make new shoes, this time using the foam rubber. This was all at my own cost, you understand, but it had to be done and not because they were wedding shoes for a princess, I would have done the same for any client for her wedding day.

The most expensive shoes I ever made cost eleven hundred guilders and were made of ostrich skin. I thought, 'these will never sell in Amsterdam, much too extravagant for Dutch people.' Our shop in Paris had just opened and I sold two pairs almost immediately.

The Woody, my 'clog shoe', is my best-selling design. A hundred thousand pairs are sold every couple of years. It earned me the Golden Clog, a sort of golden plaque from the Arthe factory in Purmerend, and to top that I also earned one guilder for each pair sold! Best idea of my life. The worst design and total flop was my Working Class Hero design, named after the song written by John Lennon. This was a flat, tough building worker's shoe with a shiny metal toecap. I couldn't give them away.

I enjoy wearing my own shoes. I don't think I could wear shoes made by anyone else. Tonny is often asked: 'are you ever unfaithful?' – but she also wears only my shoes.

Students from
the Bunka Fashion
Academy

客員教授任命書

ヤン・ヤンセン殿

文化学園に定める規定により

文化服装学院客員教授を

委嘱いたします

記

平成十七年十一月二十一日

学校法人文化学園

理事長 大沼 淳

The employment
contract (and the
English translation)
from the Bunka
Fashion Academy
in Tokyo

I use mostly calf leather, which is soft and supple. Pigskin is used for the lining. I use goat- and sheepskin as well, but not horse hide, that's for men's shoes. Horses' hindquarters make a good, useful leather. I have used snake and crocodile skin, but it's no longer necessary as perfect imitations can now be made from cow hide. No one, not even the experts, can tell the difference.

An animal must be slaughtered humanely and only for its meat, so that the skin is a by-product. Except for me, I can't do without the skin. I also make shoes for people who are allergic to leather. Here I use leather that has been tanned with vegetable oil, which prevents those with allergies from coming out in a rash.

My leather comes from Italy. The Italians have been the tanners of the world since time immemorial. The hides themselves come from Argentina, India, France and the Netherlands, but I need the Italians for the tanning. They are the true masters of the craft. They also used to be THE master shoemakers, but nowadays others have acquired the skills. In Spain, Portugal, Taiwan and China for instance. China produces millions of pairs; they can make beautiful high heels that look good at first glance. Everyone can make shoes, but tanning? Ah, that's another story. The Italians hold that particular secret, like Stradivarius with his violin.

Nowadays the Chinese have overtaken the Italians as shoe producers. Italy is experiencing the same problems that the Dutch shoe industry had in the 1970s. Then you could buy better and lovelier shoes in Italy than here, and they were also cheaper. The Netherlands just couldn't compete any more. Van Bommel no longer produces pure Dutch workmanship. The shafts come from Portugal, the stitching is done in India and they are just finished here. The craft is disappearing in the Netherlands; we are now throwing everything into shoe technology. TNO in Eindhoven is even experimenting with baking the shoes. What a bright move....developing shoe technology so that though you lose the craftsmanship, you don't just stop there, you look for something to replace it. We Dutch were the first to go into Taiwan to import Taiwanese shoes to the Netherlands. Under the motto: 'If you can't beat them, join them', instead of being a shoe producer, we had become a shoe importer. And now we've discovered technology. Well, it's an interesting development, I suppose, but I'm going to leave all that to the next generation. I'm sticking to my own last. People really ought to do what they are good at; I am still doing what I did forty-five years ago, although I confess I do sometimes make a bag or a belt from some of my remnants.

You should not be able to hear shoes coming, especially in those places where quiet is essential. I would never go to visit someone in hospital wearing leather shoes. You can hear them tapping on the floor, which is highly irritating. No, I would wear rubber soles, which are completely soundless. Schiphol airport has these smooth floors, and I wouldn't wear leather there either. Those long moving walkways at Schiphol

that carry passengers all over the place have been a source of inspiration for me. I always felt as though I was floating, and every time I was there I had the feeling that I should make a shoe that floated so smoothly. Quite unintentionally, it turned out that my floating heel was very orthopaedically correct. One of my clients who lived in Switzerland had back problems and couldn't walk in heels. She tried my floating heel, and she felt as though she were walking in flat shoes, a real liberation! She showed the shoes to her orthopaedist, upon which the erudite man concluded that I must have a deep understanding of orthopaedics. Rubbish of course, but a nice compliment all the same.

The Bruno is completely flat without a heel, or so it seems. The heel is integrated into the shoe, so although you are actually walking on a heel, you just can't see it. I designed dozens of endless variations on that model.

I am a one-man company. My accountant has always urged me to expand, but I have to put a collection together and I have always found creation more important than running a company. I've never felt the need to take on a creative assistant. I am never short of ideas, but that is not the reason: who would make the shoes that I design? Only I can do that. It would be different if I had international agents or a product manager, who could then deal with all the sales paraphernalia. But I just can't delegate, that's the problem. I still prefer to pick up all my material and deliver the finished product. Maybe I sound like a spoilt child, but the work has to be done my way, or not at all. I have never come across my ideal business partner, someone who would take over all the organization but who would not try to interfere with the creative aspects. Perhaps I do miss the boat in respect of growth and profit, but rather that than have to make concessions. A true artist doesn't water down the wine.

I am no businessman. Happily I have never been bankrupt, although I have come close a few times. I am used to hard work, I don't have any investments and we rent our house. But life is good. In America people see me in the expensive Italian or Japanese magazines. They call me and ask to speak to someone in the promotion department. 'That's me,' I reply. Then they want to talk to someone in the sales department. 'That's me too.' There's a pregnant pause, you can almost hear the disbelief 'You mean you run the whole thing?' In the Gucci factory, there is a man who is responsible only for the soles, someone else takes care of the models and then there's yet another person who just works with the leather. I do all that by myself.

I'm not rich but being a small-scale business does have its great advantages. Jil Sander was bought out by Prada and she now regrets it bitterly. That won't happen to me. Our sons will not be taking over the company; one is a philosopher, the other an architect. I don't think about getting old. I should, I suppose, but all I can think of is that I will keep on working even when I am an old man. Time is my greatest enemy and there never seems to be enough of it do everything I should be doing. I work every day. I don't have time to go to the cinema – I'm a workaholic. I sometimes take Sundays off. Then I do absolutely nothing except watch TV and have an afternoon nap. I once read that time and matter do not exist in the hereafter, you just think of something and there it is, complete. If that's true then I won't need to draw and cut a sole beforehand. Think of the time that will save.

There is plenty of young talent in the Netherlands, people who could stand in my shoes in the future! Fredi Stevens is an excellent designer, in my opinion. She makes shoes for Viktor and Rolf, but in her own style, and is innovative and refreshing. Hester Vlamings makes interesting shoes. If the demand for my shoes should ever decrease then I would still carry on designing. I simply couldn't give up, because I simply have to produce the ideas that pop into my head. The beauty of it is for me that I can hold the shoes in my hand. I have a shoe here in my office that will never be on sale even though it's made from expensive materials and represents many hours of work. My manufacturer says that I shouldn't make it, it wouldn't be cost effective! I still made the shoe though, because I wanted to hold it in my hand.

Two hundred pairs of shoes and fifty items are going under the hammer . My best-loved design is also going, the first shoes that I ever made. I cut and stitched the shoes by hand entirely by myself and even sanded the heel. 'You can't get rid of those,' I was told. But I don't feel that it's right to keep the best things for myself. But I am keeping the shoes Tonny and I wore at our wedding, and my first shoe from 1961, My call. The auction sees me waving my 'children' goodbye, but I hope that people will still be able to see them. A buyer could display them in a living room or hang them on the wall. I'd much rather see that than have my shoes hidden in a cellar somewhere or in some museum.

PHOTO PAGE 31

The cover of the

Christie's auction

catalogue

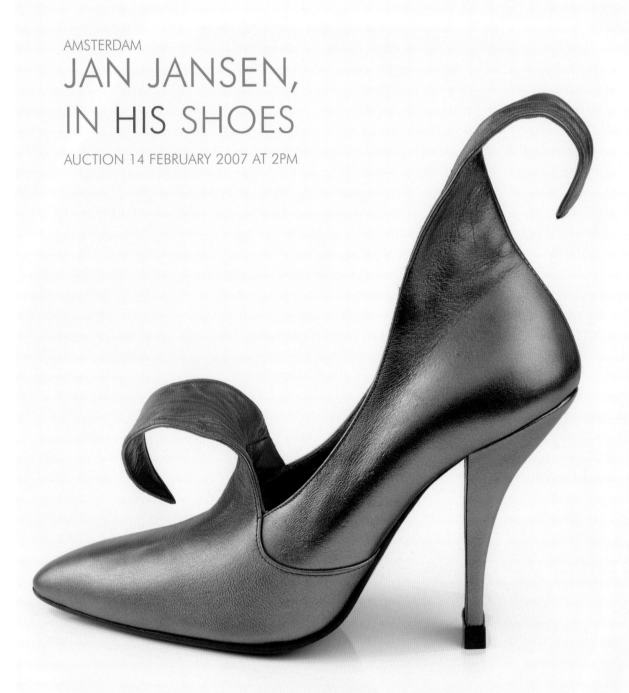

AMSTERDAM

JAN JANSEN,
IN HIS SHOES

AUCTION 14 FEBRUARY 2007 AT 2PM

CHRISTIE'S

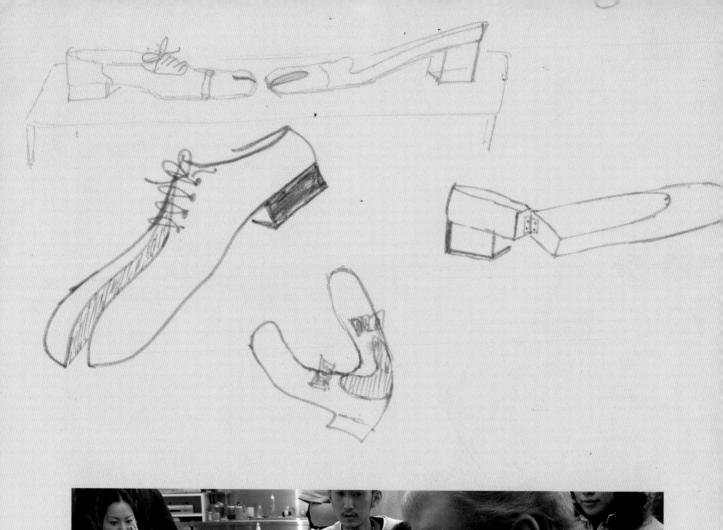

Masterclass

Before I start teaching I always tell my class: 'Close your eyes and try to visualize what you want to do with your life. Imagine for instance that you want to make shoes only for the aristocracy, or maybe design exclusively for a large commercial company. Or then again, you might imagine yourself designing only sports shoes. Now hold whatever you see firmly in your mind and concentrate on it. Open your eyes and tell yourself: "I will make this happen." Whatever it is that you really want to do is going to be what you will do best.' That is my firm conviction. I don't know what my students want for themselves; that is something they have to choose, but once I have told them what I believe, then the masterclass can begin.

Making shoes is all about making the lasts

Obviously I start by talking about the last. I want to know how they make the toe and the heel and what they would like to do differently. That completely round toe, that unconventional sole or that unusual heel form the shoe's silhouette, and these become the heart and soul of the shoe. The upper that is fitted to the last later in the process is what defines the shape and gives colour and originality, but for me the last represents the beginning and the end of the shoe. Making shoes is all about making lasts. This is what I always tell my students, whether we are in Arnhem, Milan or Tokyo. Just suppose that someone wants to make the shoe five centimeters longer. Five centimeters, that's daring! So you slap on the filler (mixed with a hardener) with a spatula, then you wait ten minutes and then start sanding. You are like a sculptor, sanding and filing the last until you get the length, width and height just right. For this you need fine and coarse sandpaper, a file and a rasp.

I also give my students technical pointers. If you are left-handed, for example, you tend to file away too much from the big toe, and leave the small toe too high. I notice this kind of thing. When the last is finished, a machine will then turn identical left and right versions, so that you can make a pair of shoes that can be fitted on both feet. This is really important because you can never be entirely sure that your design is going to work. Your drawing of the pattern and the finished last might look really fine but the proof of the design comes with the wearing of the actual shoe. When I have finished making a last I put it on top of the television set. In the evening I switch on the TV, and watch the screen and the shoe at the same time! Thoughts pop into my head: shall I make it a bit longer or just a bit shorter? Would the last look better if I add three centimeters or if I make the toe just slightly more square? It's only when I have looked at it for a couple of evenings that I will make it wider or narrower. That's when I know it's right. I was once talking to a stylist for Gucci and he told me: 'I've been in the business for eight months now and I know everything there is to know about shoes.' I told him: 'Caro imbecile! My poor innocent fool, I've been in the business for forty-five years and I still don't know all there is to know.'

Side

Front

オスドリ → メスの気をびくため

Colour

Side

Front

オスドリ → メスの気をびくため

Colour

37

Making the shoe

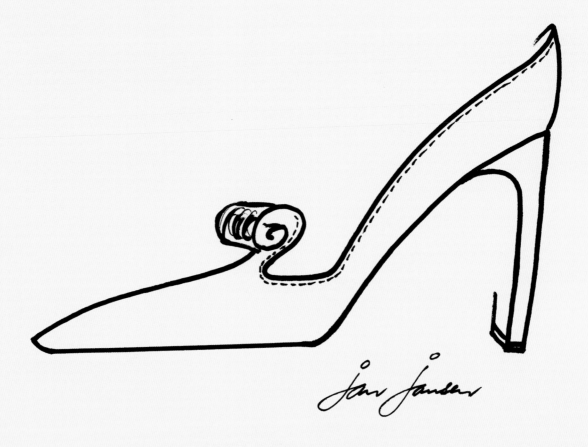

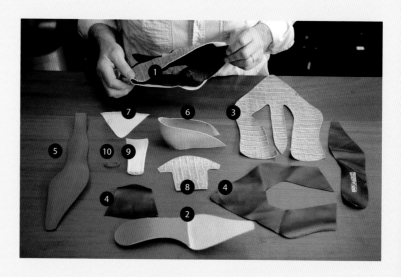

Stitched shaft (1) into which the counter-fort (6) and the toe (7) are fitted. The cut-out upper leather (3), the cut-out lining for the shaft and the sole (4), the inner sole (2), the outer sole (5), the heel covering (8), the heel (9), the running heel (10)

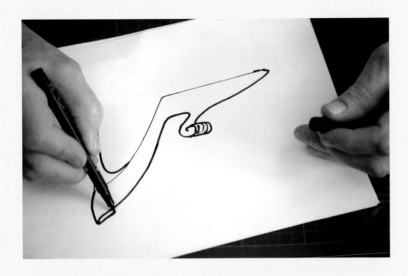

First, the design is sketched

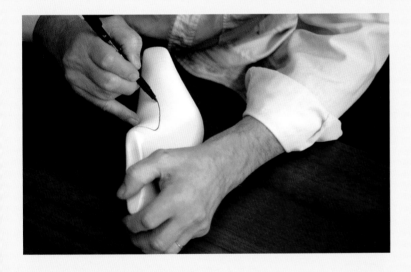

A sheet of plastic is vacuum-sealed around the last, onto which the design can be drawn. The plastic is then cut away and placed on top of a flat piece of cardboard

The pattern is placed on top of the leather and then cut out

The pattern is cut out of the leather.

Last (1), inner sole (2) and cut pattern (3).

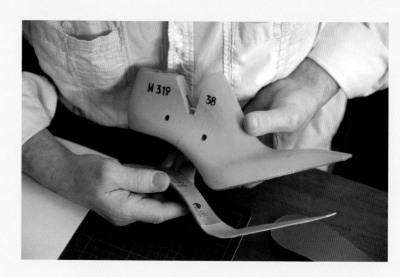

The inner sole is nailed to the last. The underpart of the last is made of metal so that the nails cannot remain upright but will bend double.

The stitched shoe is fitted onto the last and the inner sole. The back section is secured with nails while the front section is glued.

The fitting of the stitched shaft onto the last (1) and the inner sole (2) is complete.

A hinge and a hole are fitted into last. By sticking a pin in the hole, the last can be folded forwards and the shoe can be detached. The shoe is now ready.
A wire thread is fitted into the curl on top of the shoe, so that the wearer can fashion it into whatever shape she desires!

The 50 most popular Jan Jansen shoes

I have been creating shoes for over forty-five years. Although I don't know exactly how many designs I have made it must be more than two thousand.

When I'm working, I think of ideas and details that I have used in earlier designs. This makes it difficult to create any kind of timeline for my shoes; one design doesn't automatically follow another. Some designs do clearly belong to a particular era but they were not shaped by that era – they helped shape the look of that era. In the beginning, they were timeless, and I think of them as independent works of art, created by my imagination.

As far as I am concerned, my shoes are made up of shape, colour and material. I have chosen fifty examples that I feel give a summary of my work. I have grouped them in the order that I find the most suitable. It is in my head, of course, but they have actually arranged themselves.

Jan Jansen

Jan and Tonny Jansen

PHOTO Claude Vanheye

2003 | Swinging Nun

Metallic goat's leather, with an orthopaedic arch
support on a stiletto heel

Of course a nun has to go through life wearing her comfortable Birckenstock soles.

But surely even she can swing at least once in her life wearing these stilettos?

1964 | Tonny

Suede

Handcrafted by Jan Jansen

This is one of the first pairs of shoes that I ever made entirely by hand. I made the last myself and shaped the heel using a rat-tail file. This is a rasp-cut file which allows you to make these beautifully rounded arches. The only thing I hadn't quite mastered was the machine sewing – in fact I never really did. As you can see, I can only sew in straight lines; the curves are beyond me. These shoes have to be glued. Tonny tried to machine sew them, but we decided that if we want to stay together, we had better give up on that.

1993 | Norwegian Wood 2

Buckskin with a wooden sole

This design is in fact a combination of a boot and a sandal. Whether these go well together is a bit of a mystery, like in the Beatles' song after which the shoe is named: 'Norwegian Wood'. In the song, two people who are made for each other meet, but then he wakes up alone in bed the next morning and finds her gone. How did it happen?

1965 | For Dior

Corduroy, goat's leather

Handcrafted by Jan Jansen

In 1965 I plucked up my courage and went to Dior. They looked at a few designs. Some of their people thought that they were quite hideous, but they still wanted them. 'Is it possible to get paid for this?' I asked. 'Paid? What do you mean? You can say you worked for Dior.' Later the taxman came to check. 'Mr Jansen, you have worked for Dior, but we can't find any proof in your books.' They didn't believe me when I told them what had happened. 'Who works for someone without getting paid?' 'Well, it happens,' I said. I didn't think it was all that crazy!

1973 | Softline Clog

Cowhide with a wooden base

This is a mixture of everything. Sometimes my 'inventions' reappear in another form. After the success of my clog, I combined a clog with a wedge. You can't go much further with a wedge; otherwise the clog will literally fall apart. I made the shaft like those of the models in the Softline series.

1995 | My Beautiful Curls

Metallic goat's leather

With this shoe, you are wearing a collar on your heel and your instep is more like a plunging neckline. You would certainly make an entrance!

1966 | Softline 2

Patent calf leather

Handcrafted by Jan Jansen

I call this design 'Softline'. When I drew the shoes, my best pal, the painter Gustave Asselbergs said 'Hey- that's Jugendstil (the German term for Art Nouveau).' 'What's Jugendstil?' I asked him. 'I'll give you a book about it later, but first you have to finish these shoes.' There's something similar in my most recent collection. I was designing square toecaps and I drew this Jugendstil type of motif on them. 'That's not right,' I thought, 'these should be on round lasts.' But I didn't change it. It's a contradiction, but it's a visual irritation that nevertheless feels right. It's something I can't explain.

1994 | Serpent's Kiss

Python and stainless steel

I really wanted to use steel in one of my designs. It was at this time that the shoe designer Clergerie showed me how he used steel. He wanted to make sure I knew that he hadn't pinched my idea. It wasn't a great success; we only sold a couple of pairs.

2002 | Dodgem

Goat's leather (metallic and print) and suede

A dodgem car at the fair was the inspiration for this inordinately thick sole. This shoe is unique. I sold the model sometime later with a thinner sole.

1967 | Interchangeable 1

Stainless steel with a detachable brocade mule

You can detach this mule and insert a different lining, made of leather, brocade or silk for example. I call this 'interchangeable fashion'. It won me the EMS Culture Prize. I thought that this was a wonderful invention and I wanted to go into it in a big way. However, the shoe manufacturer's reaction was 'This will never sell,' even before it appeared in the shoe shops …' No one would go for it.' Now that I am a lecturer in college, I have often noticed that students are coming up with similar designs.

1979 | Indian Hands

Buckskin, with built-in wedge

I spent three weeks in Brazil designing cowboy boots. The factory also made a line of moccasins, and I wanted to have a go at them myself. I made this small bootee and the factory people thought that they were horrible! A genuine moccasin maker would have smoothed out the wrinkles. Right, that's it, I thought, this time the Indians are going to beat the Cowboys! But these little boots just didn't sell in the streets of Holland. The Bijenkorf department store eventually bought up the surplus and then they began to take off. Hundreds of thousands of copies have been produced!

1991 | Goldfinger

Suede

This is a 'chaussure fatale' – a dangerous shoe – the stiletto heel could already be deadly, but how about that toe!

1972 | Build me Up

Buckskin, with four wooden soles
covered with calf's leather

With this model you are almost designing your own shoes. The idea is based on the theme of the Woody 3. I thought: why not make the shoe higher? I added four wooden segments covered with leather. You can't actually walk on them, but I thought it was a great idea, and it was my first design to make the cover of the magazine *Panorama*. I did sell them, but using just two layers, which are as much as you can have and still lift your foot off the floor!

2002 | Garden of Eden

Scaly goat's leather

This leather with its organic blisters and scales gave me the name. It makes me think of walking through an uncultivated landscape. The hand-stitched finishing gives the impression of a garden fence.

1989 | Carnival in Venice

Buckskin on mesh

I was working on my collection in a factory one hundred-and-fifty kilometres outside Venice. It was carnival weekend and I had been invited to go but I couldn't get away. So I decided to have my own carnival by making these shoes. I went a bit over the top – you can't actually walk in the shoes but for me they are a lovely reminder of a missed weekend. I felt as though I had been to the carnival after all.

1973 | I'm Looking Through You

Mat and glossy whip snake (water snake)

I'm looking through you, where did you go

I thought I knew you, what did I know

You don't look different, but you have changed

I'm looking through you, you're not the same

In the days when I was making platform soles, I felt that I wanted to create something

lighter and less solid than the real platforms. The result was this open-work sole – it

made me think of the Beatles song, 'I'm Looking Through You'.

1982 | Thick Needles (High)

Plaited suede

At the start of the 1980s I was allowed to use the facilities of the United States Shoe Corporation in Taiwan for my own designs. Some of the women working in the factory were busy knitting and I had a sudden inspiration – I could make shoes and boots using this kind of craftwork! Eventually some of these designs appeared on the European and American markets and were very successful.

1994 | Hot Winter Night

Lambskin

Imagine: a hot winter's night; lying on a sheepskin rug in front of a real fire, drinking wine and wearing these boots....

1989 | First Aid

Buckskin with EVA sole (a kind of plastic)

I once saw a very sexy nurse giving first aid. The straps of her sandals were so narrow that her heel kept sliding off the sole. Then I had a vision of these sandals. Oh, if only she could have worn them!

2001 | Turn me On (High)

Goat's leather

When you look at the shoe pattern laid out flat, you can see that a part in the middle would normally be cut out and thrown away. With this curly shoe, you use the whole piece of leather instead of cutting away the middle bit. A piece of wire is inserted in that section so that you can curl the flap whichever way you fancy. I made four stilettos for this shoe and it's still in the collection. It has become a classic.

1977 | High Heeled Sneaker

Canvas and goat's leather with a rubber sole

In 1977, I received a commission from a manufacturer who wanted to do 'something big'. He told me that he had brought Levi Strauss to Europe, and he wanted me to do something in the shoe and clothing line. The clothing was designed by Berry Brun, under my supervision. I made the shoes but they were never actually produced, or at least, not here. An American manufacturer launched them under his own label without my permission – and he sold more than one million pairs!

1995 | Turn my Beautiful Curls

Metallic goat's leather

Seducing with a curl – that's the idea behind this shoe. It is a variation of My Beautiful

Curls. This is more chic, it's more daring. The curls are more voluptuous.

1995 | Grasshopper

Metallic goat's leather

I made this shoe on the same last that I used for the Tania. The shoe looks completely different when you use another base. I do use many different kinds of lasts but when the shape works, you should leave it at that.

1978 | Working Class Girl

Patent leather

I designed a flat men's shoe and named it after the John Lennon song called 'Working Class Hero'. It had a prominent steel toecap for the tough construction worker. This is the woman's version; *high heels for tough girls*. No-one got the point but they still sold. They fit the description in the professional literature of *punk, but without the anarchy*… or words to that effect.

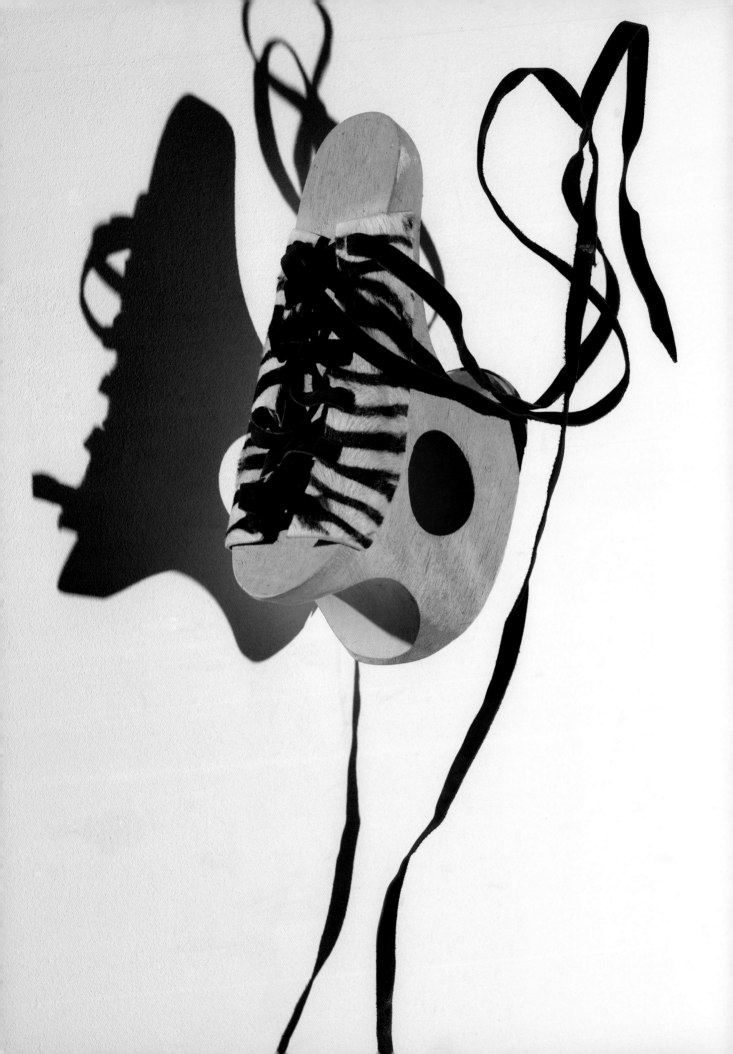

1994 | Unfinished Business

Furry calf's leather in a tiger print

This is actually a *shoe in the making*, and is nowhere near finished. I wanted to make something with a wooden sole and came up with the idea of a wedge. But you can't stand up in these shoes, you'd just fall over. So I fitted a piece of sole leather under the heel. I just left it at that. Sometimes I leave things for years before picking them up again.

2000 | I'll Always Love You

Goat's leather with suede

This is such a successful shoe that it has never been equalled. That wedge heel is so comfortable! My customers say that that is the Jan Jansen feeling. Sometimes the wedge is in fashion, sometimes it isn't, but I still keep making it.

1979 | Kiss Me on the Couch

Goat's leather

I once saw a Salvador Dali exhibition at the Boijmans Van Beuningen Museum in Rotterdam, and it made a huge impact on me. When I saw Dali's sofa, which was inspired by Mae West's lips, I just knew I had to make these shoes! These insoles really pamper a woman's foot. It's as though you are nestling on Dali's sofa or against Mae West's satin lips. I did add something, though – the tip of a tongue is sticking out from the lips! Cheeky…

1973 | Rattan

Buckskin, bamboo and a crêpe sole

At the start of the 1970s, my clogs were a huge success. Everyone told me that I should widen my horizons, so I applied for the Semaine du Cuir (Leather Week) in Paris. This meant that I had to come up with a design that would make everyone sit up and take notice. This is when I came up with the idea of the bamboo shoe. We were on holiday in the south of France at the time and I sat up at nights drawing. After three weeks of serious headaches, I suddenly realized that I had been sitting on a bamboo chair. It was a light-bulb moment. Why couldn't you walk on bamboo? It became one of my most talked-about designs. For years afterwards, and even now, people refer to me as 'the bamboo shoe man'.

1996 | Tiger

Hand painted linen by Ella Koopman

Hand crafted by Jan Jansen

The artist Ella Koopman asked to make something using her fabrics for the 'Fabric in Form' exhibition in the Town Hall in The Hague. She wanted to show how her fabrics could be used in different ways and forms. Observing the rhythm and structure of various surfaces is second nature to her, and I knew I could really do something with this. I moulded the fabric onto one of my lasts without using a pattern – the last is still in there.

1980 | Mirror on the Wall

Suede, with transparent plastic

Mirror, mirror on the wall, who is the fairest of them all? If a woman has a lovely foot you shouldn't try to cover it up, it ought to be on show – and so I came up with this 'see-through' design. It was just an experiment really; I just wanted to try it out. It never went into production so this is the only example – a shoe that only fits one foot. But that's a different fairy tale.

1995 | Avenue's Best Cover

Metallic goat's leather

The legendary *Avenue* was the first Dutch glossy magazine. I thought that this shoe simply had to be on the cover. So this is what happened – and it was the best cover *Avenue* ever published. I think so anyway.

1981 | Not Interchangeable

Transparent plastic, suede insole, metallic goat's leather and buckskin

I had my own factory in Italy for a while. My business partner Aldo Binarelli could make anything! But then I created a design that really tested his limits. I wanted a walking boot and a Wellington boot combined, but I thought that it would be impossible – but he did it. You have to admire the man. The factory depended to a large extent on the production of this boot for quite a while.

1989 | Love

Goat's leather, metallic leather with a
floating wedge made of ABS rubber

This is the first floating wedge that I designed and made, this is where it all started.
The balance is superb. As Tonny said: 'You could run a tram on these.' There are some
people who simply can't walk in heels but they can walk in these shoes. One of my
customers asked her orthopaedist: 'Why is it that I can actually walk in these shoes?'
The orthopaedist replied: 'This man understands orthopaedics.' That's ridiculous – it
was pure luck.

1994 | Flo-Jo

Buckskin, metallic goat's leather and an EVA sole

This was designed for Florence Griffith-Joyner, or Flo Jo, the American athlete with the long nails. She held two world records in 1988 and broke the Olympic record. She was in the Netherlands to record a TV programme and was being thoroughly feted. The TV channel that had invited her asked me to design a pair of shoes especially for her. When I presented them to her I said: 'You've already got three gold medals – here's the fourth. If you compete in these, you'll have a head start.' She loved that.

1991 | Salvatore

Suede, with a filled insole

I deliberately used only the Christian name here. There is one famous and one not-so-famous Salvatore: Salvatore Ferragamo and Salvatore Deodato. I admire both these shoe designers tremendously, and this shoe is my homage to them both.

2000 | For Snoecks

Suede, patent leather with a vulcanised sole

There is an American designer called Beverly Feldman who makes very 'busy' shoes. Under the soles is the legend *too much is not enough*. I must have been thinking about that when I designed these shoes. My very good friend Swip Stolk was designing some pages for *Snoecks* in the year 2000 and asked me to make something crazy, that I wouldn't actually put on the market. Voilà.

1974 | Fong Leng 2

Suede, metallic and silver goat's leather

Mathilde Willink had a passion for Fong Leng's clothes and for my shoes. She was always talking about 'our Jan'. She then asked, 'Would you make me a pair of shoes?' Carel Willink liked Mathilde best in laced-up boots. I pointed out that it took an awfully long time to get them off. But he enjoyed that too, it seems, so I made a pair of lace-up boots for her (or rather for him).

1991 | What is This?

Suede

In some Islamic traditions, it is the custom that when a girl menstruates for the first time, her father gives her a pair of 'grown-up women's shoes'. But as they will be size twenty-fives, she is not expected to actually wear them, they just symbolise the transition. I designed these shoes for one of those girls. Although I made them in 'grown-up women's sizes', the little girl was the inspiration. So that's this one!

1997 | Truck

Patent calf's leather

It was those fantastic American lorries with their shining, high metal grills that inspired me to come up with this flattened shoetree design.

1970 | Fong Leng 1

Suede, metallic and gold goat's leather
with a layered sole

I would never have made this kind of shoe if it hadn't been for Fong Leng's shows.
I knew Fong's clothes and she knew my designs. She let me create the wildest designs
for her shows – she gave me full rein. I really enjoyed working with her.

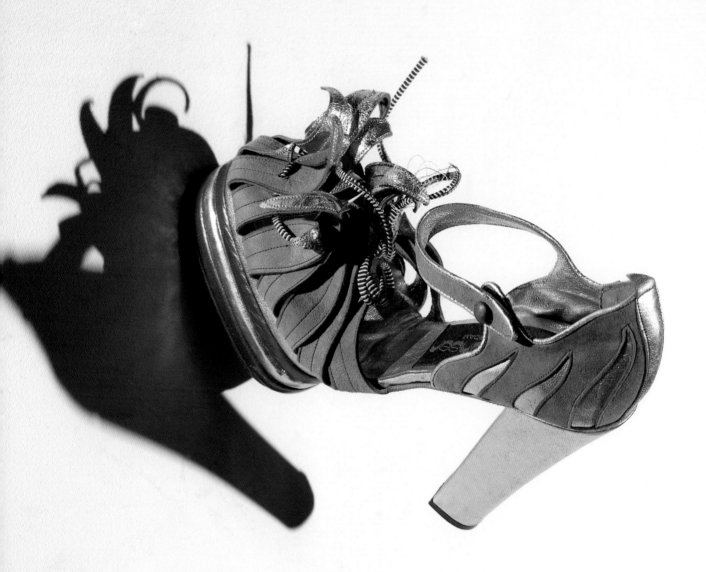

1985 | Shelter

Suede with a sheepskin lining

I call this system Aeroline, and have used it in various designs, including the Shelter. I can't remember how I developed this system. When you are designing, you draw the model on the last. The modeller, the patternmaker ought to stick to the last, but now I actually enjoy working beyond the last. It's difficult to mould a piece of leather without using a last, you just don't know how it's going to turn out. With this shoe, I let the customer decide how it will look; there are all kinds of ways to wear the shoe. Tonny is still discovering different ways to fold and tie the flap.

1990 | Pussy Galore

Metallic goat's leather with rabbit's fur

Pussy Galore was the Bond girl in *Goldfinger*. At the start of the film she has to be handled with care, but of course in the end she falls for James Bond's charms. And he for hers.

1978 | Brazilian Highway

Buckskin, metallic goat's leather
and Brazilian toadskin

When toads want to mate they prefer to return to the pool where they were born.
The males are lazier than the females and hitch a lift on the backs of the females when
they can. Actually this male still does that.

1994 | Rio

Metallic calf's leather, plywood,
wood and a plastic base

Carnival in Rio and all those dancers from a samba school wearing these sandals –
what a sight that would be …

1975 | Foot Balance

Nappa, brushed metallic goat's leather,
elastic and hairy calf's leather

Frans Haks called this the 'leaning heel'. I find the voluptuous shaft in perfect balance
with the heel and the platform. This shoe is still worn in a play by an actor playing
Satan.

1995 | Stir my Blue Blood

Patent calf's leather and metallic goat's leather

James Bond prefers his martinis 'shaken, not stirred'. This shoe is finished in Moonraker

Blue, a metallic sky blue. Worn by the right woman, this is the perfect weapon to get

James Bond moving.

1973 | Plywood Poker

Plywood sole with a raffia upper

I once watched a carpenter punching holes in plywood to use in a cupboard, and I suddenly had an idea. I got the same carpenter to make this sole out of a piece of plywood. It is a unique sample, as I never put it into production.

1991 | Derrière

Suede and goat's leather

My first production shoes were made in a factory in Loon op Zand. I once designed a shoe with a bow on the heel. I can still hear the manufacturer's words: 'Jan, the fancy bits should be at the front – no one will want a bow at the back. But still, have it your way.' It's always been like that. As you can see!

1989 | Merel

Metallic patent calf's leather

Merel, oh, that was simply the best. A crackled metallic patent leather with a high ankle strap. I just loved making this 'bombé (bulbous) sole'. This shoe is still being worn, by Annemarie Oster for example.

1998 | Barely - Merely

Calf's leather, with a plywood base

The lower sole was made for a particular model but the top wedge was designed for another shoe. The two together make an unusual combination. I only ever made one pair of these. The other half of the pair is in the Leather and Shoe Museum in Offenbach am Main, Germany.

... I know that I'm good. Not long ago I dreamed that there was a new shoe designer in the Netherlands and he was absolutely brilliant. I could see his shoes right in front of me. A genius. I suddenly realised I had become a nobody. Then I woke up. And that shoe designer didn't exist. But his shoe was brilliant, and I had it in my head. I had only to draw it.

Jan Jansen in *Vrij Nederland*, 24th August 1974

Biography | Jan Jansen

1941   6th May
Johan Boudewijn Marie Jansen was born in Nijmegen, where his father was the sales
manager for the Nimco children's shoe factory.

1947   6th May
Jan Jansen made his First Communion.

*Six years old. My First Communion, and I had to wear these hard, horrible shoes. With an
absolutely straight face, I told my father that there had to be a way to make these shoes
more comfortable and more elegant.*
De Telegraaf, 18th July 2004

1960   Jan Jansen did his military service after finishing secondary school. At the weekends
he worked in a shoe shop in Nijmegen.

1961   Through his father's connections, Jan Jansen started his training in September as
a shoe designer. He did his apprenticeship in the Pallas shoe factory in Nijmegen.
He learned how to make patterns in the Neerlandia Schoenfabriek (shoe factory) in
Loon op Zand, where he was earning *f* 50,– a week.

PHOTO PAGE 148
Roy Beusker

Jan Jansen
kneeling at the
communion rail

Jan Jansen
aged nineteen

Me, hand made
men's shoes, 1961

Neerlandia taught me how factory designs were created from beginning to end: when representatives would see a lovely shoe somewhere, they would take it to the design department and ask them to create something similar.
Vorm & Industrie in Nederland, 1984

Jan Jansen designed the first pair of shoes in his collection in Loon op Zand: a pair of black men's shoes. He made the shoes in his own size, 41.5 (7.5 UK size), something he still does today with all his designs for men's shoes. The stitching is done in the factory because Jan doesn't know how to sew. He does the rest himself.

Jansen soon became recognised for his quality designs and began to sell his designs for ƒ 25,– per sketch to the Empress shoe factory. He went to night school at the Shoemakers' School in Waalwijk and the Industrial Design Academy in Eindhoven.

1962   The director of Empress, Charles Porocarrero, offered Jansen a job as a designer. The salary that he was offered meant that Jan Jansen was able to get married. His girlfriend Tonny Polman advised him to follow his dream, and to go and study in Rome. In exchange for his designs and the latest news from Rome, Empress offered to cover his living costs in Italy. Jansen considers his decision to go to Rome as a pivotal point in his career.

The editor of the magazine *Schoenvisie* (Shoe Vision), Aimée van Tricht, made it possible for Jan to work at various workshops in Italy, including Follie, D'Alco and Albanese. This is where he saw the lasts for Sophia Loren and Audrey Hepburn. Everything was done by hand. Jan Jansen diligently took notes of everything that was going on and in the evening he repeated everything he had seen in his room. Albanese allowed him to experiment on the old lasts using remnants.

1963   When he came back to Holland, Jan Jansen set up his own business in his parents' cellar. He got engaged to his childhood sweetheart Tonny Polman, the woman he calls his muse.

I work closely with Jan and read everything I can about shoes and types of leather etc.
Tonny Polman, 1963

In April 1963 set up his own workshop at 16 Jonge Roelensteeg in Amsterdam, above an arts and crafts shop.

In Nijmegen, where I lived, they thought [...] I was a bit strange, an outsider. Tonny, who was then my fiancée, struggled with that attitude as well. I still remember designing a pair of rather striking boots for her, which provoked quite an aggressive reaction from some people. They said things like 'Hey, where's your horse?' Or 'Why don't you go to Russia?' We both found this extremely annoying, and that's the reason we moved to Amsterdam. That was quite an experience.
Trouw, 23rd August 1974

1st October
Jan Jansen registered his company with the Chamber of Commerce. The registration read: 'designing ladies' and men's shoes, manufacturing shoes according to own design, ladies' and men's shoe shop and shoe wholesaler.'

1964   Out of admiration for the French shoe designer Roger Vivier, and also because he wanted a posh name for his shoes, Jan Jansen chose the trade name Jeannot Haute Chaussure, also known as Jeannot. The name is a combination of Jean (Jan) and -not (Ton, from Tonny, backwards).

PAGES 152-153
The 'Craftmanship is Mastery'
Grolsch campaign
PHOTO Paul Huf

Quite by chance, Jan Jansen met Paul Huf, who was taking photos for the Grolsch beer advertising campaign running under the slogan 'Craftsmanship is Mastery'. Huf was impressed by Jan Jansen's workmanship and his exclusive designs. A photo showing Jan Jansen in his workshop became part of the Grolsch campaign.

Wedding photo
of Jan Jansen and
Tonny Polman,
Nijmegen,
20th June 1964

Paul Huf advised Jan to organise a press show for his work, and this had an immediate impact. Jan's work was noticed by the couturiers Dick Holthaus, Max Heijmans and Frans Molenaar.

8th May
Jan Jansen took part in a fashion show with Dick Holthaus and the hair stylist Mario, at the opening of a hairdressing salon in Zandvoort. His beach sandals and boots were a huge success.

Shoe designer steals the show with his designs.
Haarlems Dagblad, 9th May 1964

20th June
Jan Jansen married Tonny Polman and they went off to Paris for their honeymoon. Jan introduced himself at Dior and was promised that the Paris fashion house would use his designs.

See pages 50-51

In the same year, Jan Jansen sold twenty designs to the Carel company. The shoes were used as part of the Christmas window display in the company's store in Paris.

Headline in
De Telegraaf,
25th April 1964

1965
Up to 1965 Jan Jansen was making just a couple of pairs of each of his made-to-measure shoes. From that year onwards, his designs went into small-scale production (five to six pairs).

2nd February
Jan Jansen held a press show with twenty-five samples, made by the manufacturer Hadley in Loon op Zand.

foto's: PAUL HUF

Jan Jansen maakt haute chaussure

door ERNA VAN DEN BERG

AMSTERDAM, zaterdag.

AMSTERDAM is een handwerksman rijker geworden: een schoenontwerper. Niet voor mensen met moeilijke voeten, maar voor vrouwen, die een haute chaussure voor hun voeten wensen. Jeannot noemt Jan Jansen zijn zaakje op de eerste verdieping in de Jonge Roelensteeg, dat vandaag officieel wordt geopend.

Jan Jansen is 22 jaar. Een leuke jongen met lachende ogen en een prachtige rij tanden. In zijn spraak schuilt de zachte g. Hij komt uit Nijmegen. Daar heeft hij het vak geleerd. Na zijn middelbare school ging hij modellen ontwerpen voor verschillende schoenfabrieken. Hij wilde de Nederlandse confectieschoen meer elan geven. Maar zijn ontwerpen leverden nog wel eens moeilijkheden op voor de produktie. Dan werd er iets aan veranderd. Als dat gebeurde, was voor Jan Jansen het plezier eraf. In die tijd is bij hem het idee geboren om zélf schoenen te maken. Enkele stuks voor vrouwen aan wie dit besteed zou zijn. Maar wie leert je zo iets in een land waar aangemeten schoenen alleen een noodzakelijke luxe zijn voor mensen met moeilijke voeten?

Naar Rome

BIJ ging ervoor naar Rome, naar het atelier van Follie. Na twee maanden wist hij hoe hij de schoenen, die hij in zijn gedachten had, met zijn handen moest maken.

Toen was er nog maar één wens: een atelier in Amsterdam. Een jaar lang heeft hij zich stilletjes op de openingsdag van vandaag voorbereid in het 2-bij-3-meter-kamertje boven een kunstzaakje. Een hele smalle wenteltrap leidt naar het kleine schoenenpaleisje. Uit zijn met stof beplakte dozen haalt hij enkele schoentjes te voorschijn. Juweeltjes van zacht leer of stof, met stompe neuzen en elegante hakjes. Eén paar is helemaal versierd met kleine kraaltjes, als de muiltjes van Assepoester...

Grootvaders

ZE zijn geboren in het brein van deze 22-jarige, gekleed in een spijkerbroek en een gestreept hemd. Een jongen, die het — door onze vaders verstoten — handwerk van onze grootvaders weer opneemt om te maken wat hij mooi vindt. „Ik geloof, dat er in deze tijd van mechanisatie behoefte is aan goed handwerk", vindt hij zelf. „In Italië en Frankrijk hebben de mensen veel geld over voor ontwerpschoenen. Ik ben ervan overtuigd, dat er in Nederland ook zo'n groep is. Er zijn hier zoveel goedgeklede vrouwen en het lijkt me dat die niet alleen haute-couture, maar ook haute chaussure willen. Het is alleen vervelend, dat het Nederlandse klimaat mijn vak enigszins tegenwerkt. Want als je hier 's morgens de deur uitgaat, weet je nooit wat voor weer het 's middags zal zijn. Maar volgens mij kan de Nederlandse vrouw dat oplossen door altijd een extra-paar schoenen mee te nemen in de auto of in de tas."

Paar dagen

JAN JANSEN gelooft in de verkoop van zijn schoenen, die bepaald geen paar tientjes zullen gaan kosten. Heel begrijpelijk trouwens, want het maken van één paar schoenen kost hem een paar dagen.

Of de Nederlandse vrouw al aan haute chaussure toe is? Als ze de schoenen hierboven ziet, zal ze alleen maar ja zeggen. Er is trouwens ook een man die dit al gezegd heeft: Dick Holthaus. Deze week zag hij voor het eerst de schoenencollectie van Jan Jansen en deze chaussure past zo bij zijn couture, dat er ogenblikkelijk plannen zijn gemaakt voor de najaarscollecties.

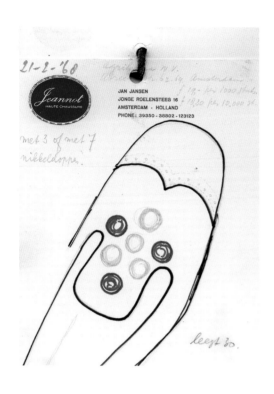

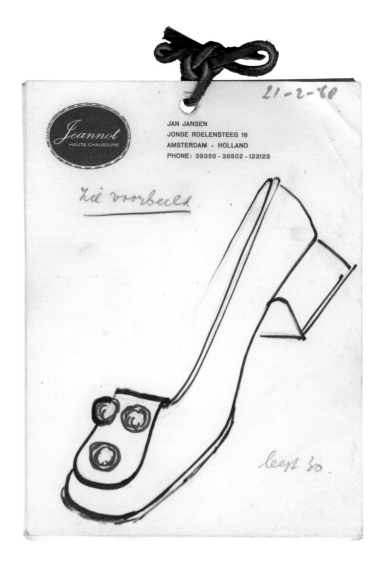

Sketches showing
the Jeannot heel

Jan Jansen's Jeannot heel became an icon in the shoe world.

Meanwhile, Jan Jansen sold his designs to twenty-two shoe outlets, including Bata International, De Lange and Hessels.

I think it's wonderful that especially the young people who love my shoes but don't have much money are now able buy them.
Elegance, 1965

1966
See pages 56-57

Jan Jansen designed the Softline shoe, whose heels were made by the Beerens shoe factory in Loon op Zand. The painter Gustave Asselbergs noticed that there was an affinity with Jugendstil, although Jan was unfamiliar with this style.

PHOTO PAGE 157
Jan Jansen with the
Softline shoes, 1967

The Jeannot Softline collection is youthful and revolutionary…
Het Binnenhof, 26th March 1966

21st June
The birth of his son Olivier.

28th October – 4th December
The Softline shoes were included in the 'Atelier 4' exhibition at the Stedelijk Museum in Amsterdam.

20th November 1966 – 15th January 1967
Jan Jansen's designs were shown at the international 'New Shapes of Colour' exhibition at the Stedelijk Museum in Amsterdam.

1967   From 1967 the trendsetting magazine *Avenue* regularly featured Jan Jansen's work. His designs were shown in the Dutch Pavilion at the World Fair in Montreal, Canada.

Jan Jansen received the EMS Culture Fashion Award in The Hague for his latest design, the Interchangeable.

Jan Jansen in front
of his shoe shop
in the Runstraat

1968   12th January – 18th February
Along with three other designers, Jan Jansen took part in the 'Current Fashion' exhibition at the Stedelijk Museum in Amsterdam.

Bla bla in het Stedelijk […] Grote uitzondering hierop: Het werk van schoenontwerper Jan Jansen, de enige die naar mijn mening aanvoelt wat de toekomst inhoudt ...
De Telegraaf, 20th January 1968

Bla bla in the Stedelijk […] With one notable exception: The work of shoe designer Jan Jansen, who in my opinion is the only one with any feeling for what the future holds ...

The appearance of an article in *Dépêche Mode* marked the first time Jan Jansen was recognized in an international magazine.

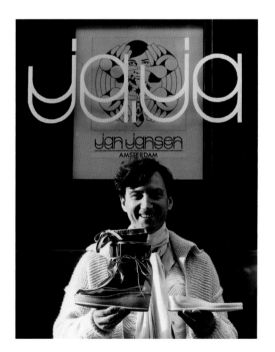

Il hasarde des jeux audacieux de textures et de couleurs, de perspex et d'acier inoxydable. Encore de la sculpture à porter (He plays outrageous games with textures and colours, Perspex and stainless steel. Once again we have wearable sculpture!)
Dépêche Mode, August 1968

Jan Jansen started to work with the large shoe factory Jacques Bergmans, which would go on to produce limited editions of Jan's designs for the next three years.

28th June
Jan Jansen opened the JaJa shoe shop at 4 Runstraat in Amsterdam. The interior of the shop was designed by Kho-Liang-le, while the designer Swip Stolk made the new logo for the shop and for the shoes. The manufacturer Jacques Bergmans, who had enormous faith in Jan, financed the new shop and the stock.

Jan Jansen has opened a shoe shop. Finally!!!!!!!!
De Telegraaf, 28th June 1968

olland
erald

NEWSMAGAZINE OF THE NETHERLANDS/
VOLUME 8 NUMBER 11

november 1973

YOUR KLM COPY

Going
to
the
clogs

The Woody designed
by Jan Jansen on
the cover of the
Holland Herald,
number 11, 1969

1969   Jan Jansen added designs for men's shoes to his collection.

I started to make men's shoes because of the huge demand – and I thoroughly enjoyed it.
Algemeen Dagblad, 26th September 1969

The creation of the Woody clog. The clog was made by Knoek and Ros in Bunschoten, which was a subsidiary of the Timtur factory in Waalwijk. Timtur also worked for Mary Quant and Jan Jansen. The Woody became one of Jan's most-imitated models. Amongst the imitations was the one made in 1971 by the French designer François Villon for Yves St. Laurent.

1970   The Woody went into large-scale production at the Arthé factory in Purmerend, but when Arthé could no longer keep up with the demand after the first three years, production was switched to Italy. Woodies could also be made-to-measure by Bert and Truus Luiken in Kaatsheuvel. They left one side of the Woody so that it wasn't fastened to the sole, so that it could be nailed to fit the individual measurements.

Jan Jansen is unique in the Dutch shoe world. Thank goodness that the Dutch shoe industry
is beginning to take notice. The shoe industry should be honouring him as the only true
cobbler left in Holland.
Schoenexpress, 27th February 1970

1971   The Woodies were also a great international success. From the winter of 1970 they were on sale at Russell & Bromley's in London's West End.

Jan Jansen has been creating these kinds of shoes for a couple of seasons. It is scandalous
that he has had more success in England than in his own country.
De Volkskrant, 10th February 1971

Jan Jansen started lecturing at the Arts and Industry Academy in Enschede.

1972   21st May
The birth of his son Lok (Laurens).

See pages 68-69   Jan Jansen made an exaggerated version of the Woody for his summer collection. Various undersoles could be attached to the platform in different colours. The tallest Woody has five layers and is 10 cm high. These were sold at Studio Fong Leng in Amsterdam.

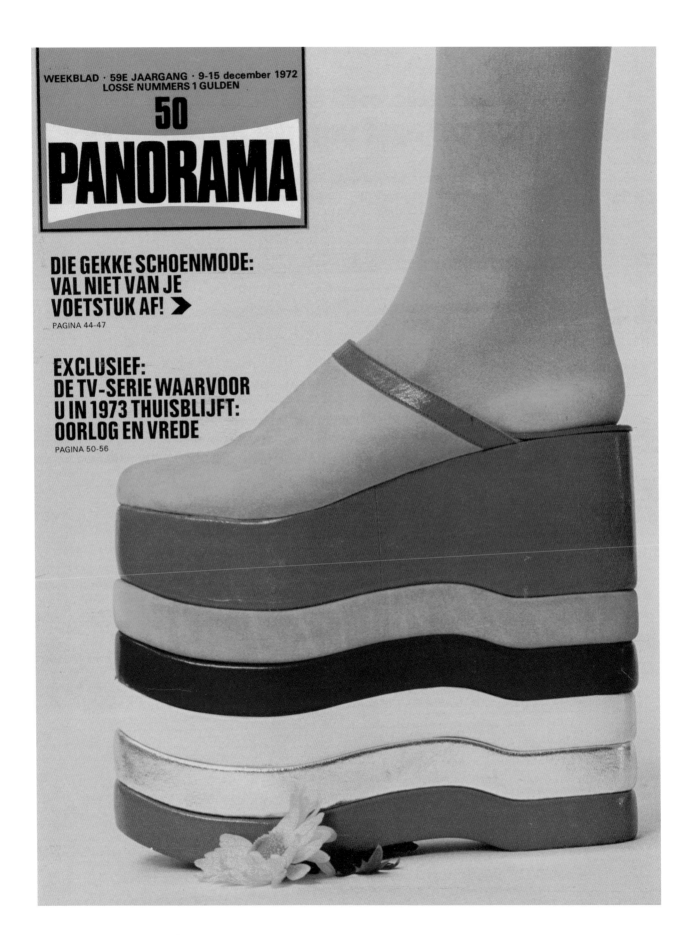

WEEKBLAD · 59E JAARGANG · 9-15 december 1972
LOSSE NUMMERS 1 GULDEN

50

PANORAMA

DIE GEKKE SCHOENMODE: VAL NIET VAN JE VOETSTUK AF! ➤

PAGINA 44-47

EXCLUSIEF: DE TV-SERIE WAARVOOR U IN 1973 THUISBLIJFT: OORLOG EN VREDE

PAGINA 50-56

Build me Up
on the cover of
Panorama magazine,
December 1972

In 1972 Jan Jansen made a series of shoes called Dutch Trimming. Each half of the shoe was made in a different colour.

Jan Jansen on uneven but colourful feet.

Het Parool, 28th April 1972

1973

See pages 98-99

The collector Frits Becht advised Jan Jansen to take part in the French Leather Fair in Paris, and lent his support. For this international debut, Jan created the Rattan, a shoe that had an open platform, with a heel made from bamboo, hence its nickname 'the bamboo shoe'.

The interest shown in the Dutch couturier Jan Jansen had a lot to do with his stand: a perfect reproduction of the oldest profession in the world on the Quayside in Amsterdam.

Set Magazine, 26th October 1973

Jan Jansen's stand,
French Leather Fair
Paris, 1973

Star of the recent French Leather Fair, Jansen is likely to become an international house-hold word by next spring. What will do it is his super summer sandal, quite simply built like Victorian colonial furniture out of varnished rattan cane.
The Daily News, 4th October 1973

The American shoe chain Edison Brothers ordered twelve hundred pairs of the bamboo shoes to use as decoration in their stores, but Jansen couldn't deliver on time because of production problems.

1974   The royalties from de Woody enabled Jan Jansen to ask the Rohé Company to develop the bamboo shoe. As he couldn't find anyone in Holland who could manufacture the shoe, it was made in Italy from the first half of 1975. It was officially launched at the Bijenkorf department store in Amsterdam.

The success of the bamboo shoe meant that Jan Jansen was offered freelance commissions from Charles Jourdan, Multishoe of New York, Block van Heyst in Holland and the Spanish firm Garcia, to name but a few.

Cruyff de los zapatos, un Holandes llamado Jansen. (The Johan Cruyff of the shoe world – a Dutchman called Jan Jansen.)
Diaro de Elda, 18th March 1975

Fong Leng's show
in the Van Gogh
Museum,
14th November 1974

Jan Jansen designed shoes for Fong Leng Tsang's shows. The first show, 'Fashion in Art', was held on 14th November 1974 in the Van Gogh Museum.

See pages 116-117

and 122-123

Praise for both Fong Leng and Jan Jansen, who made sure that Amsterdam had a fashion show the likes of which it has never seen. Let's hope it's not the last.
De Volkskrant, 15th November 1974

21st August – 6th October
'Jan Jansen's shoes from 1964 - 1974'; was the name of the exhibition at the Central Museum in Utrecht. The Stedelijk Museum in Amsterdam also honoured Jan with their exhibition: 'Ten years of Jan Jansen'.

Jan and Tonny Jansen
at the 'Jan Jansen's
shoes 1964 -1974'
exhibition

1975

Jan Jansen receives
the 'Golden Clog'

13th March
Jan Jansen received the 'Golden Clog' from Arthé, on the production of 100,000 pairs of Woodies. Jan Jansen received royalties of ƒ 1,– for each pair sold.

The Bijenkorf department store started selling the bamboo shoe, which was then being manufactured by the Italian company Rafaello Galgani and which cost ƒ 89,–.

1977

See pages 84-85

Jan Jansen designed the High Heeled Sneaker for Falcon, which is a co-operative made up of Macintosh, Europe's largest ready-to-wear clothing producer, and Cosmia BV, a shoe importer in Amsterdam. This co-operative didn't last long and the production was taken over by the American importer Carber. Eventually more than one million pairs of the High Heeled Sneaker were sold.

1978   Jan Jansen was still designing for haute couture as well as the production line. He designed the D'Jays for the Dutch importer Van Drunen, which were based on the moccasin and the opanque, the traditional sandal from the Balkans, and were made in Brazil. The D'Jays did not take off straight away. The Bijenkorf department store offered them in brightly coloured buckskin. In the end they were a great success and many illegal copies appeared on the market.

From the end of 1978, Jan Jansen had his own production line in a small factory near Florence: Calzaturificio Jan Jansen e C. snc. He set this up with an Italian partner, Aldo Binarelli. The workforce could turn their hand to anything, even to making the bamboo shoes.

I wanted to be able to make everything that I could possibly make, maybe fantastic ballerina pumps one season, and gold platforms the next. All in the height of fashion, of course.
Set Magazine, 14th September 1979

1979   As Jan Jansen had predicted, high heels came back into fashion. For the Spring collec-
See pages 96-97   tion of 1979, his designs included the Kiss me on the Couch, a luxurious erotic shoe.

I enjoy designing heels best of all.
Haagsche Courant, 12th March 1980

The shoe shop in the Runstraat received a makeover, designed once again by Swip Stolk. Jan Jansen wanted the design to be inspired by the café atmosphere interior of Edward Kienholz in the Stedelijk Museum in Amsterdam.

PHOTO PAGE 169
Jan Jansen with his family inside the shoe shop in the Runstraat. In the shop you will meet the 'eternal customer', a shop-window dummy sitting at the piano, who will be happy to make way for anyone who wants to play 'live'..
PHOTO Hans Bakema

1980 18th January – 9th March

Designs by Jan Jansen and other shoe designers went on display at the 'Fashions in Fashionable Clothing' exhibition Museum in Amsterdam. They were also included in the London Crafts Council's 1981- exhibition 'The Shoe Show, British Shoe Designs since 1790', which was a touring exhibition in collaboration with the department responsible for the circulation of State Collections.

1981 Jan Jansen designed the Bruno, a men's shoe with a flat sole which came in a variety of colours. Right from the start, the Bruno was also worn by women, including the Dutch girl group the Dolly Dots. This shoe is the most copied of Jansen's designs to date.

23rd December 1981 – 7th February 1982
Jan Jansen took part in the exhibition 'Aspects of shape, eleven designers', in the Fodor Museum in Amsterdam.

1982 In 1982 Jan Jansen met Norman Finn, who was in charge of production for the United States Shoe Corporation. He enabled Jan Jansen to make use of the facilities of his design department in Taiwan. This is where Jan created the Knitted Boot and the elasticised ladies' shoe, of which more than 30,000 pairs would be sold by the Bijenkorf department store.

See pages 76-77

Jan Jansen's invitation to the Modacalzatura Trade Show in Bologna, 1982

1983   Jan Jansen moved his shoe shop from the Runstraat to number 42 Rokin in Amsterdam. He sold only shoes made under his own name. Swip Stolk designed the interior, which graced the front page of the Japanese magazine *European Shop Designs*.

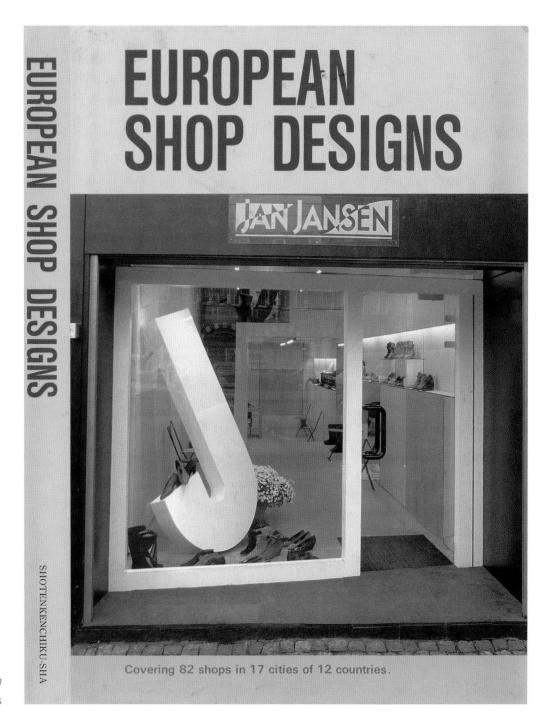

Cover of *European Shop Designs*

An advertisement
for Jan Jansen in
Interview, Andy
Warhol's magazine,
dated April 1983

Jan Jansen designs were also popular in America. ETF Enterprises of New York imported Jan's shoes, hoping to attract younger customers.

A young, contemporary line by Dutch designer Jan Johnson. [sic]
Footwear News, 3rd May 1982

1984   Some Jan Jansen designs from the 70's became bestsellers in the 80's, such as the Zippy from 1979. He took his wife Tonny's advice and started production for his own shoe shops. After several seasons, copies appeared everywhere on the market. Jan himself estimates that the number totalled over a million. More than 500,000 pairs were sold each season in the USA.

1985   The city of Amsterdam presented Jan with his first award as fashion (i.e. shoe) designer, namely the prestigious Kho Liang Ie-prize for industrial design. He received the ƒ 10.000,– prize for his entire work since 1964.

Jan Jansen belongs to the handful of international designers who can still work independently under their own names.
NRC Handelsblad, 13th September 1985

An unusual Jan Jansen design from 1985 is the Aeroline. This shoe has a large flap that can be made into different shapes according to the wearer's whim.

Presentation of the
Kho Liang Ie-prize to
Jan Jansen

1986   15th November 1986 – 4th January 1987
        The Stedelijk Museum in Amsterdam organised the exhibition '22 Years Jan Jansen
        Shoe Designer'. The exhibition also went to Emmen and Waalwijk at the beginning
        of 1987.

The interior of
Jan Jansen's shoe
shop in Paris
        One of Jan's dreams came true when he opened a shoe shop on the Rue des St. Pères
        62 in Paris, THE street for Parisian shoe designers. Paris loved his designs.

        *Chaque chaussure imaginée par le createur hollandais Jan Jansen est tantôt un moment
        d'émotion, tantôt un fou rire, un élan de luxe, un coup de pied aux conventions.* (Every
        shoe created by the Dutch designer Jan Jansen is sometimes a moment of pure
        emotion, sometimes a giggle, a moment of luxurious ecstasy, a kick in the face of
        convention.)
        Gap, June 1988

        In 1986, Jan Jansen was invited by the United Nations as a guest lecturer at the Aca-
        demy for Industrial Design in Havana, Cuba.

1987   22nd September – 18th October
        Jan Jansen took part in the 'Mode du Royaume des Pays-Bas' exhibition at the Dutch
        Institute in Paris.

1989   Jan Jansen introduced the Floating Wedge. Earlier versions of this design were too
See pages 108-109   weak. The design appeared on the cover of Ars Week, a professional shoe journal.

        *La scarpa senza tacco. Un' altra creazione uscita dalle abillissime mani di Jan Jansen e
        destinata a rimanere nella storia dello sviluppo tecnico della calzatura.* (The shoe without
        a heel, yet another creation from the talented hands of Jan Jansen, who deserves to be
        included in the annals of technical development in the shoe industry.)
        Ars Week, 5th April 1989

        Jan Jansen received the Emmy van Leersum-prize
        for fashion design from the City of Amsterdam.

1991 *Linea Erotica in* *Vogue-Pelle,* *November/* *December 1991*	Jan Jansen received a freelance commission from the German manufacturer of the BAMA orthopaedic shoes. This gave him the idea of an 'erotic' collection: pumps with high heels. This was the start of the Linea Erotica. *Architetture da Calzare, Jan Jansen. Dall' Olanda, scarpe 'erotiche e stravaganti'* (Architecture that you can wear by Jan Jansen from Holland, 'erotic and extravagant' shoes) *Vogue-Pelle*, November/December 1991

1992	The City Fashion Museum in Hasselt organised the exhibition 'A dance of shoes in the Fashion Museum, shoes from 1900 to the present'. To his amazement, Jan saw a shoe with a floating heel made by Salvatore Ferragamo in 1947.
1993	Jan Jansen's designs were shown in the 'Die Verlassenen Schuhe' exhibition in Bonn, at the Rheinisches Landesmuseum. Jan Jansen is the living shoe designer with his own museum exhibition. His 'Derrière' design graces the cover of the exhibition catalogue.
See pages 58-59	Jan Jansen used flexible steel in organic shapes as a heel in his Steely Snake and Serpent's Kiss designs. *They are sculptures, the models that go beyond fashion. Materials bend docilely to the form: steel flexes and becomes a heel, balanced by the python-covered platform.* *Ars Week*, December 1993

PHOTO PAGE 177

The cover of the
catalogue of
Die Verlassenen
Schuhe

DIE VERLASSENEN SCHUHE

Avenue

1994	Jan Jansen designed a pair of shoes
See pages 110-111	for the athlete and Olympic champion
	Florence Griffith-Joyner, or Flo-Jo.

1994

See pages 110-111

Jan Jansen designed a pair of shoes for the athlete and Olympic champion Florence Griffith-Joyner, or Flo-Jo.

1995

The Tania model designed by Jan Jansen was chosen by Linda O'Keeffe for the dust jacket of her book *Shoes: A Celebration of Pumps, Sandals, Slippers and More*, New York, 1996.

See pages 104-105

Photograph of Florence Griffith-Joyner with the text: 'To Jan Jansen, thanks for the beautiful shoes, love, Florence Griffith-Joyner'

In her article 'Futuristic Fit' in *Vogue*, the photographer Inez van Lamsweerde used many of Jan Jansen's models.
One of Jan's designs photographed by Inez van Lamsweerde appeared on the cover of *Avenue*.

In 1995 Jan Jansen opened a shoe shop in Antwerp at 38 Huidevettersstraat.

PHOTO PAGE 178
Cover of *Avenue*, number 2 from 1995
PHOTO Inez van Lamsweerde

The cover of *Shoes: A Celebration of Pumps, Sandals, Slippers and More*, New York, 1996

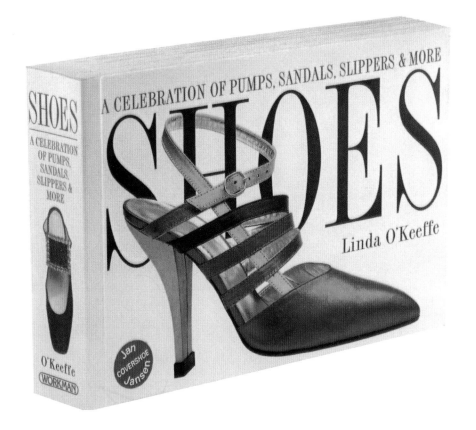

1996

See pages 100-101

Jan created new designs for the 'Fabric in Form' exhibition at the Gemeentemuseum in The Hague, which included the Tiger. He used hand painted linen by Ella Koopman.

Together with Jack Wiebenga, Jan Jansen launched the Jan Jansen Sense line. He wanted to offer ready-to-wear shoes at a reasonable price to a larger public.

Jan Jansen received the 'Grand Seigneur', the most prestigious Dutch fashion award. The award was presented by Mrs Van Dok-Van Weele, the Secretary of State for Economic Affairs.

Taking part in the 'Design and Identity, Aspects of European Design' exhibition at the Louisiana Museum of Modern Art in Humblebaek, Denmark.

Jan and Tonny Jansen at the 'Grand Seigneur' award ceremony

The cover of the
catalogue *Jan Jansen,*
Master of Shoe Design

Jan Jansen and
Swip Stolk
PHOTO Josée van Dijk

2001   Swip Stolk gave Jan's shoe shop on the Rokin a makeover.

2002   9th February – 20th May
Jan Jansen was honoured with an exhibition at the Gemeentemuseum in The Hague
entitled 'Jan Jansen, Master of Shoe Design'. To coincide with the exhibition, a publication of the same name was produced which showed Jan Jansen's work to date. Joop
and Janine van den Ende and Paul Mertz were responsible for the exhibition and the
publication and Swip Stolk designed the layout.

25th August – 20th October
The 'Jan Jansen, Master of Shoe Design' exhibition was held at the German Leather
and Shoe Museum in Offenbach am Main, Germany.

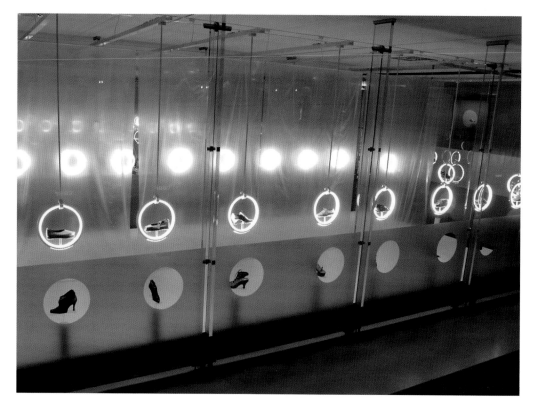

Design of the
'Jan Jansen, Master
of Shoe Design'
exhibition

In 2002, Jan Jansen was given the Oeuvre Award by the Sculpture, Design and Architecture Foundation.

17th October 2002 – 2nd February 2003
Jan Jansen's work was shown at the 'Chaussés-croisés' exhibition at the Museum of Contemporary Design and Applied Arts in Lausanne, alongside designs by Manolo Blahnik, Pierre Cardin, Salvatore Ferragamo, Roger Vivier and Vivian Westwood.

2003   Jan Jansen received the Oeuvre Award from the ANWR, one of the largest shoe purchasing cooperatives.

2004   The 'Jan Jansen, Master of Shoe Design' exhibition travelled to Japan and could be seen at six museums between March 2004 and May 2005. The exhibitions, held in Shibuya, Kyoto, Kushiro, Minamitsuru-gun, Nishinomiya and Kitakyusyu-shi were designed by his son Lok Jansen. The exhibition attracted 50,000 visitors.

Eclectic Dutch shoe designer Jan Jansen is taking his wacky shoes on the road.
Footwear News, 2nd February 2004

Jan and Tonny Jansen
at the Parco Museum
in Shibuya, Tokyo
PHOTO Aramaki

During the exhibitions in Japan, Jan gave masterclasses for up and coming shoe designers.

Flyer for the Parco
Museum exhibition

ぜんぶ、奥さんの、ためだけに
作った靴なの？すごい！

Jan Jansen / Master of Shoe Design

オランダが生んだ靴の魔術師 ヤン・ヤンセンの世界展

PARCOMUSEUM of art and beyond

2004年3月20日[土]ー5月9日[日] 会期中無休 ／ 開館時間10:00−20:30（入場は20:00まで）最終日のみ19:00にて閉場

Jan and Tonny Jansen
with students from
the Bunka Fashion
Academy

184

2005   Armani launched a copy of Jan Jansen's 1994 Tutti Piedi shoe design. The courts ruled that Armani should take the shoe off the market.

The Italian fashion titan Prada put a copy of the bamboo shoe on the market. They were not sued.

2006   Jan Jansen became a professor at the Bunka Fashion Academy in Tokyo, and a guest lecturer at the Ars Arpel School (vocational training for shoes) in Milan.

27th April
Jan Jansen received the 'Max Heijmans ring', which is awarded every two years to someone who has made an exceptional contribution to Dutch fashion. The award was presented by the Association of Dutch Fashion Journalists.

Jan Jansen teaching
at the Ars Arpel
School in Milan

Jan Jansen
accepting the
Max Heijmans ring
from the designer
Frans Molenaar

2007   Jan Jansen is now sixty-five, and has been a shoe designer for forty-five years. He has more than two thousand designs to his name and his innovations have revolutionised the shoe industry. He still works without a fancy studio, together with his wife Tonny. His shoes are sold in his shoe shops, Jan Jansen Shoes, in Amsterdam, Heusden and St.Ives (United Kingdom). He also takes on freelance work for international shoe houses. It is impossible to say how many of Jan's shoes are being worn, but it has to be in the millions.

14th February
Something like two hundred-and-fifty of Jan's designs were auctioned at Christie's Auction House in Amsterdam, including many unique pairs of shoes, in the hope that they would find their way to those who love and collect Jan Jansen's shoes.

Jan and Tonny Jansen
in their workroom

PHOTO Masayuki Aramaki

I first met Jan in 1958 and married him in 1964, which means of course that we have been married for forty-two years. I have to say, looking back, Jan hasn't changed at all – he is still the designer filled with enthusiasm that he always was. He is still that mischievous, romantic and altogether lovely young man. When we are sitting in a restaurant he always makes sure that I have a seat with the best view. Quite often during dinner or a meeting I see his eyes glaze over; and not just for 'split seconds', but for several seconds, you understand! This is how I know he's working again, and if I ask him if he has seen anything, sometimes he'll say yes, or he will draw something, sometimes he won't say anything at all. But I know he'll have created a new design for his next collection. When he has a new design I am always so proud when he asks: 'Take a look at this with your carpenter's eye, what do you think? You can improve the design.' And sometimes I do. Jan is no womanizer, but when you look at his collection then you know that here's a man who adores women. I am so thrilled that he calls me his muse.

Tonny Jansen, 2007

PHOTO PAGE 189

Jan and Tonny Jansen
in the 1970s

PHOTO PAGES 190-191

Inez van Lamsweerde and

Vinoodh Matadin

© 2007
Publisher: Terra Lannoo BV
P.O. Box 614, 6800 AP Arnhem
the Netherlands
info@terralannoo.nl
www.terralannoo.nl

The publisher Terra belongs to
the Lannoo Group, Belgium

Text: Tonko Dop, Lucas Bonekamp
Translation: Textcase, Hilversum
Design: Studio Jan de Boer, Amsterdam
Illustrations editor: Lucas Bonekamp
Photos of shoes pages 44-143: Niels Schumm
and Anuschka Blommers
Cover photos pages 32-33, 144-145: Roy Beusker
Photo page 2: Anna Beeke
Photo page 6: Lok Jansen
Photos pages 38-41: Bob Bronshoff
Lithography: Pixel-It, Zutphen
Printing and Binding: Trento Printer, Italy
Editors: Janine van den Ende,
Maarten van Nispen and Patricia Kok

ISBN 978 90 5897 725 0 (English edition)
ISBN 978 90 5897 724 3 (Dutch edition)
NUR 452

This publication was made possible by

VandenEnde
FOUNDATION
ARTS & MEDIA

With thanks to: Viktor & Rolf